C'ing Your Way Clear

Every Woman's Guide to Handling Life's Storms

TOYA L. EVANS

Haci Publishing
PO Box 2111
Ashburn, VA 20146

Manufactured in the United States of America

Please visit my website at
www.changethings2day.com for information

Library of Congress Control Number: 2007903731
ISBN Number: 978-0-9794475-0-1

Bookcover design by Nicole Rogers

Edited by Lynn M. Taylor

Proofreading by Wheknown Jasper-Booker and Gloria Strong

Layout and Design by Delaney-Designs

Website Design by Desiree Denmon –www.Emaginesolutions.com

ACKNOWLEDGMENTS

I will look to the hills from whence cometh my help –
all of my help cometh from the Lord…
Psalm 121 (KJV)

Thank you God for my storms for without them, how would I grow and enjoy the favor you desire for my life? The chasm I had to cross in this recent storm has truly been a blessing. While I initially saw it as an ending, you showed me what a new beginning it was. Thank you for helping me "C" my way through it.

God, in His infinite wisdom, places just the right people around you at the right time in order that His purpose may be fulfilled. I would be remiss without thanking those people who have encouraged me to complete this project in the midst of my own storm – Stephanie E. Williams (friend, partner and confidante), Jerel Eaglin, Cavell Johnson, Traci Bahsoon, Glenda Roberts, Andrew "Tripp" Jones, Terrill Atkinson, Dr. James L. Graham, Rev. Robin McCoy, and all my long-time friends who allowed me to pitch my idea and concept to them, and offered candid advice about its potential.

Ted Jordan – you are the best Dad and since we met, you have ALWAYS had my back. I love you much. Dallas Atkinson (RIP) – I know you are watching over me. You taught me so much in my life and I will never forget you. To my uncles who have always felt like big brothers – Lemm (RIP), Pop (RIP), Larry (RIP), Jimmy and Lamont – you have always been the wind beneath my wings and I thank you for it. To my family members (you may not have a direct "shout out" but you know who you are) thanks for all the love.

Gerald Levert (RIP), Mary J. Blige, Rizen and Fred Hammond, your music has been soothing to my soul in a time of storm. Barbara Crump, thanks for being a friend and all your help with Sister Moments. Patricia Robinson-Mitchell of Projecting Images - thank you for your press and publicity assistance. RLS – I'm glad God placed you in my life. Thank you for setting the standard and for sharing my love for the power of words.

To the "change agents" – all the women who shared their stories for this project – simply put, thank you. Without you, this project would not be possible. I must say listening to and capturing each of your stories was very moving to me. Some of you planned to tell me one story and then once we got going, the Spirit led something else to flow. Your willingness to be transparent continues to be confirmation that God wants to use us to bless so many. I thank you for opening up your life and your heart so that others might benefit.

Last, but certainly not least, I need to thank the key women in my life — my daughters, Lauren and Chanel (keep doing what you do), my mom, Linda Jordan and my grandmother, Juanita Atkinson. You are a constant source of inspiration to me and always allow me to be me. I love you forever.

DEDICATION

This book is dedicated to the memory of Monique Nicole Sherard Oliveri
(October 12, 1965 – June 20, 2006)

PREFACE

Several years ago I found myself in the middle of a personal and professional crisis – one that I didn't see coming on any fronts. Or did I? Had I ignored the signs for too long when the winds of change and challenge were all around me? In order to restore some sense of peace and order in my life, I began to keep a journal — writing poetry and general thoughts. One night I woke up and began to jot down words that started with the letter "C". I wasn't sure why they were coming to me this way but I captured them anyway. Several days later the thought came back to me again and I began to play around with the words once again. I thought, "Wow this could be a series of poems, writings, etc. I need to do something with this." There was so much excitement and many ideas began to flow about the direction the project could take. I continued to capture it all in my journal.

However, like many of us, when the storm winds blew over, I returned to my normal routine and my journal unfortunately became a casualty. For more than 5 years, I made no entries at all – that is until a huge storm caught me off guard and I sought solace again in my writing. What overwhelmed me was that I had been given a vision long ago to proceed with the project and had done nothing with it. I decided that the time had come. My season had arrived. I would act on the vision that had been given to me in 1999.

This time I thought about ways to enrich the message. What better way than to incorporate the stories of real, everyday women? I refer to the women who shared their amazing stories with me as "change agents" because, through their actions, they were victorious over a dark period in their lives – loss of a child, caring for an aging parent, incest, abandonment, addiction, and more.

I invite you to journey with me through the eyes of these "change agents" and embrace their experiences. I assure you it will be moving and life changing for you. And just when you may have thought you were the only one to experience a rough patch in your life, you'll soon realize that there are so many others who have traveled your road already and made it through. My work on this project has given me a fresh perspective on the power that is within each of us to create calm in a storm.

TABLE OF CONTENTS

INTRODUCTION

What is a storm? Dictionary.com defines a storm as "a violent disturbance of affairs...." Ever felt overwhelmed by the circumstances around you? Ever felt like the rug was pulled from underneath you? Ever felt that whatever you were going through only happened to you and that you were all alone? Most of us have been in at least one or more of these situations. But Ecclesiastes 1:9 says: "What has been will be again, what has been done will be done again; there is nothing new under the sun," meaning we are not alone in the challenges we face because the challenge has been experienced by someone else before.

The purpose of this book is to encourage every woman in a personal crisis by showing that change is possible. The stories of other women's struggles through divorce, death, fear, and abuse (to name a few) are intended to inspire you to keep going and know that victory is attainable. When you are willing to face difficult life experiences, work through them and love your way out, you will gain greater confidence to handle your next challenge.

The seven chapters in this book imply a sequential set of steps to clear a storm. However, the reality is any of the "C" steps can be a turning point to C'ing Your Way Clear. In each chapter, motivational/inspirational quotes from historical figures, notable therapists and stories from "change agents" provide helpful insights. Additionally, personal exercises have been designed to navigate you through tough situations. These exercises will lead you to look inward. Use them to evaluate where you are, your thoughts about it and what victory feels like for you. Let them be your source of inspiration and aspiration as you work through your storm – knowing with full assurance that it will pass, you will clear, and emerge for the better.

In a recent sermon, Dr. James L. Graham, Pastor of Mount Pleasant Baptist Church in Herndon, VA, stated, "Storms may be on your itinerary but peace is your destination." With that thought in mind, let this book be one of your roadmaps to becoming more than just a survivor, but an achiever, who is no longer bound but free. It is my hope that regardless of your religious beliefs, you will see God as a saving grace in each story.

CHAPTER 1

CONSULT GOD

God will either give us what we ask, or what He knows to be better for us.
Saint Bernard

Max Lucado in his book, <u>Grace for the Moment</u>, suggests that in order to heal, we must take the first step. Whatever our needs are "God's help is near and always available, but it is only given to those who seek it." As women who may have been reared to take charge and get things done, coming to terms with our lack of control in a situation can be frightening. When we are in trouble, our first instinct is to do something to fix it right away.

The first source of help should be God. Why do we sometimes overlook Him? Because we believe that either we or someone else has the answer to our problems or requests. It's as if we are saying to God – "I Got This. I know how to take care of this." What arrogance we demonstrate! We forget that regardless of the situation, small or great, God doesn't need our help. As a result, we find ourselves in the storm longer than necessary, simply because we forget or just don't go to God and ask for help.

The inability to let go and focus more on the promise God has for us than the pain we are experiencing keeps us in an endless cycle. In times such as this, author Kathy Troccoli suggests we seek humility. In her book, <u>Live Like You Mean It: Seven Celebrations to Rejuvenate Your Soul</u>, she says humility allows us to be teachable and gives us power "because you are teachable enough to hear God and go to higher places with Him."

The moment we admit we are not in control and release our concerns to God, there is peace. The surrender allows us to get out of the way and seek God for His care so He can release His covering, protection and restoration. Psalm 23:1-3 reminds us "The Lord is my shepherd; I shall not be in want. He makes me lie down in green pastures, He leads me beside quiet waters, He restores my soul." What a promise! No matter what the situation, we can ask God for help and He will do what He said He would do.

"Not My Will but His Will be Done" – Michelle's Story

I had always considered myself a strong and intelligent person. I've always lived my life on my own terms and no one or nothing could control me. So how could I become addicted to drugs and alcohol for more than 15 years? How could I let my life go on a downward spiral? How did things get so out of control so fast?

After high school, I joined the military, began to drink more frequently and experimented with different types of drugs. At the age of 23, I found out that I was infertile and went into a deep depression. Drugs, for me, became a way to numb my pain. What I thought was a casual pain killer, quickly became a habit. Before I knew it, I was addicted to cocaine.

Even after falling in love and getting married, the pain was still there. I could not accept my infertility nor could I shake my cocaine habit. My life began to deteriorate year after year. Drugs kept me numb and became a part of my daily routine. I began to feel like a loser for becoming an addict and at times, I felt like I would never be anything else. I kept getting high and it cost me in every part of my life – divorce, unemployment, and eventually homelessness. I hit rock bottom and was tired of living that way. I was tired of hurting. I was tired of numbing my feelings. I knew I had to get help. Believing I was in control, I had tried many times to get clean on my own, but each time I failed. For a long time I didn't think I had a problem. In my mind, I was ok and *everyone else* had the problem. I couldn't admit that I was sick. I was in denial.

Then God stepped in. In a moment of clarity, I realized that I was tired and something had to change. I decided to seek help. I thought of a family member who had gotten clean and I had enough faith to believe that if God could clean her up, He would do the same for me. After praying for strength, I called her and she helped me get into a treatment facility and a 6-month structured halfway house. During my time in the halfway house I found a temporary job and took advantage of all the resources available to me. I began to see how God was working in the lives of others and it kept me encouraged.

Half of my battle was turning my life, and especially my will, completely over to God's care. The good news is getting clean and surrendering to God changed my life for the better. Once I gave control of my life to God, I began to love myself again and learned to live life on life's terms. I began to believe that God loved me unconditionally. I felt better equipped to deal with things that haunted me from my past. I learned to deal with my emotions and do it all without drugs or alcohol.

I believe everything I've endured throughout my life has been for a purpose. That purpose is to give God glory. Through tear-drenched cheeks, I used to constantly ask "why"? Why did I have to experience drug addiction? Why couldn't I have children? Why did I have to go through a divorce? I finally have the answer to all those questions – for the glory of God.

The temporary job God blessed me with while I was in the halfway house turned into a permanent position. It's been seven years and I am still working in the same department today. Since I have been there, I have earned the respect of my colleagues and earned three promotions. I also have remarried, purchased a home with my husband, and joined a wonderful church. I love the new person I've become and I have joy in my life today.

I give all honor and praise to God. I believe the testimony of my experience has and will continue to help others who are traveling down the road I traveled. I have no shame sharing my story with others because I believe that's what God wants me to do. This is why He saved me. I asked Him for help and He brought me through so that someone else would believe that they could also come through. God is not a respecter of persons. If He did it for me, He will do it for someone else. Some days I get stubborn and want to take back my will. I have to remember that I am not in charge. God is. I have to remember – not my will but His will be done and I am so very thankful.

"Be Still and Know That I am God"
– Jill's Story (alias used)

Emotional separation is painful. Sometimes you don't realize the void it causes. But, I had to do it. I separated myself from my mother; the one person that I thought *should* or *must* love me.

Not many people know that I was adopted as a young child. I knew my father loved me dearly and unconditionally. We were best friends and I always enjoyed the time I spent with him. I thought my mother loved me too until my teenage years. Growing up, my sister and I were not allowed to spend the night out at friends' homes. However, I wanted to stay with a friend from high school and I begged my parents to get to know her family so they would agree to a sleepover. They finally gave in. My friend arranged for a double date with some guys. That night, I lost my virginity and became pregnant.

I wasn't aware of the changes going on in my body. My mother never talked to me about sex. She just said, "Don't do it." I didn't feel comfortable talking to her about what was going on so I confided in an Aunt hoping she would give me some guidance or tell my mother for me. She refused so I went for weeks without telling anyone else. One day my mother confronted me and I was glad. I no longer had to hide anymore. I thought, at least she knew and would help me. This wasn't the case, however, and it was the beginning of the end of our relationship. It was the wedge that would separate us for a lifetime.

The change in my mother's behavior was immediate. She did not hide her disappointment and became very cruel. We lived in a 4-level row house. She made me constantly walk up and down the stairs, carry buckets of water to the washing machine and take baths in all types of chemicals and concoctions. She wanted me to abort the baby, which scared and confused me. I finally asked her "Do you Love Me?" I couldn't see how since she was subjecting me to such treatment. She never responded to my question. The hurt I felt from her lack of response was heartbreaking. At that point, I felt I had no other choice but to leave so I ran away from home.

I called my father and he said, "I don't care what happened, just come home." When he came to pick me up, I told him about the baby. He immediately began to worry about my mother's reaction. I didn't have the heart to tell him that she already knew. I also couldn't tell him how she treated me. He told me that if I wanted to keep the baby he and my mother would help to raise it. He also said if I wanted to have an abortion I could do that too. It was my decision and he would support whatever choice I made.

When we got home he told my mother about the pregnancy and she pretended as if she didn't know. She never told him about all her efforts to force me to lose the baby. I felt safe and relieved that both of my parents finally knew because I really wanted to keep the baby and needed their support to get through the pregnancy. However, my father's support didn't last long. My room was near my parents and I could hear the arguments between them. My mother wanted me to have an abortion and nothing else. She constantly badgered my father to agree to the abortion. Eventually, he gave in to her and came to me with an ultimatum. If I wanted to remain in the house with my parents, I had to have an abortion.

The woman they arranged for me to see was very mean. Her disappointment reminded me of my mother. After the procedure was over, the strange woman put the aborted fetus in a jar and brought it back to me. She placed the jar in my face and told me not to do "it" again or this would happen again. I was horrified. The terror of that day was so traumatic that I put it out of my mind and never spoke about it again for more than 30 years.

When we returned home no one ever mentioned my pregnancy, the cruelty, or the abortion again. It was as if nothing ever happened. But something did happen and my relationship with my mother was never the same. I felt betrayed by her behavior and was left with emptiness. I was emotionally devastated and decided to part ways with my mother.

At the time, I wasn't spiritually mature enough to know where to look for help. I didn't know that in the absence of my mother's support, I could have the love and support of the Heavenly Father. He was always available to me. Through the years and other personal trials, I am grateful that I have developed an intimate relationship with God. This was a turning point for me. I now know that God will not let me "fall by the wayside" and He will comfort and fill up all the emptiness inside of me. I also realize that I have to ask for the help I need.

Each day I feel closer to Him and depend more on His grace and favor. The antidepressants I once depended on are becoming a distant memory. I have entrusted my concerns to the Lord. Through prayer, I am becoming stronger and stronger.

Despite a few bouts of depression, I am making it through without medication. I have forgiven myself for the mistakes I made. I am a witness that when you cry out to God for help, He will hear your cry and deliver you. I have learned just to "be still and know that He is God."

"A Lesson in Life" – Syreeta's Story

A'mira Tune was a gift from God. Her life lasted only 45 days and yet she taught me so much about life in the time she was here. I accept God's purpose for her life and it has made the difference in mine. A'mira was my first child and I was excited for her arrival. I had a premonition that she would be born early. However, I never expected her to come as early as she did.

At 26 weeks, A'mira arrived — the result of a placenta abruption that caused pre-term labor. I was very afraid that she wouldn't make it. She needed more time in the womb to grow. I felt there was nothing I could do but turn my situation over to God. I prayed and asked others to pray for me. Her health was declining quickly and the possibility of her survival and leading a normal life was slim. I began to wonder, "Why is this happening?" I was praying but not at peace.

When I finally accepted that A'mira was destined to be on earth for a short time and that her death was inevitable, I found peace. In the midst of my circumstance I realized that A'mira belonged to God and her death was His will. By seeking God's counsel, I found victory in my storm. I feel grateful that God allowed her to be a part of my life for the 45 days that she was here. Instead of focusing on the time we didn't have together or the memories we didn't get to create, I am thankful for the time we did have and what A'mira taught me. I appreciate life and the gift of motherhood even more now. I know that God is preparing me for something else and I can't wait to see what it is!

Lessons Learned

- God is always present and ready to give us comfort and peace.

- God doesn't need our help in any situation – we must "let go and let God".

Exercise for the Day

1. Make a list of the things you stand in need of.
2. Recite the following prayer to God. Insert the items from your list:

God I am tired of trying to _____ my way.
I need your help. Speak to me and give me the strength to
be obedient to your direction.

CHAPTER 2

CONFRONT YOUR FEARS

You gain strength, courage, and confidence by every experience
in which you really stop to look fear in the face. You must do the thing
which you think you cannot do.
Eleanor Roosevelt

What causes fear — lack of information, false perceptions, the unknown? While some of our fears are inherent by nature, others are learned. For discussion purposes, the focus of this chapter will be on learned fears. These types of fears are the ones that keep us from being all we can be in life. They might develop out of a negative experience, a failure, a bad relationship or an uncomfortable situation. Whatever the cause of the fear, holding on to them, remaining in a comfort zone, or not taking a risk can be toxic. Fear can stop us from achieving our goals and aspirations. Often times when we are afraid, we talk ourselves out of doing something before anyone else can.

In her book, Fearless Living, Rhonda Britten suggests that "fear stands between you and your ability to go anywhere you like, do anything you want, and meet anyone you please. To help you stay safe, fear motivates you to hide your essential nature by thwarting your ability to express yourself truthfully." It is the concept of truth and our inability to face it that sometimes keeps us in fear. We ask ourselves - If people knew the real me would they still accept me?

The book, <u>When Things Fall Apart: Heart Advice for Difficult Times</u>, by Pema Chodron defines fear as "a natural reaction to moving closer to the truth." And why would we shy from the truth? What is it about the truth that would frighten us? Without the truth we cannot be free. John 8:32 states "Then you will know the truth, and the truth will set you free."

Facing the truth allows us to understand our fear, the power we have given to it and the effect it has on our life. The truth allows us to identify challenges, imagine the possibilities and rid ourselves of heavy "fear" baggage that we carry around. Highly successful authors Jack Canfield and Mark Hansen (Chicken Soup for the Soul series) suggest in their book <u>The Power of Focus</u> that "if you want to gain confidence, accelerate your progress, and restore your energy to maximum levels, you must confront your fears."

"And When You are Free" – Toya's Story

The very first man in my life was nicknamed "Mack." I'm not sure why my dad had that name but in today's times it seems fitting for him.

He was a good-looking man who already had four of his seven children at a young age – the first four children were by three different women. He must have decided that it was too much for him because he headed West, leaving his children and I'm sure "baby mama drama" behind. For whatever reason, personal contact and financial support were limited.

I was in elementary school before it really hit me that I didn't have a traditional family setting. My mom was in New York working, my dad was in California and I was in North Carolina with my grandparents. No one knows how and why fear takes up residence and I don't know at what point the thought of being left behind made such a difference in my life.

I was a "superstar" in my family – doted on by all of my uncles and my grandparents. There were never any threats from anyone in my family and yet I felt as if I wasn't "good", somehow my world would change and the people I loved would leave me. My journey to being the best at absolutely everything began and so did my effort to be as mean to my dad as I could. Why shouldn't I? I felt he abandoned me and that hurt me more than I even knew at the time.

This fear manifested itself in my relationship with my husband of over twenty years. One man had already left me and I was scared to death of being left by another one. Unfortunately, my husband recognized my weakness and used it to try to control me. He would say to me on many occasions what I hadn't heard as a young child but always felt — "we can always go our separate ways." Those words would paralyze me. I didn't recognize my husband's own insecurities. I thought it was just me. To keep him from leaving I would work harder, do more of what I thought he wanted, (trying to figure out how to fix me), argue and try to fight —anything so I wouldn't be left alone.

My husband and I generally had two versions of our marriage – "very good" and "very bad." There never seemed to be a middle ground and I never seemed prepared for when it would turn from good to bad. I was always caught off guard. This started to wear me out. During the final "very bad" time, I got a call from my dad and I lashed out at him in a way that I hadn't done in the past. I typically tried to stay as far away from him as possible and limit our conversations and interactions. After we hung up, I asked myself "why did I answer the phone?" I cried myself to sleep that night. Sometime during the night, I had a dream that I was talking to my grandfather. I felt my ankles shaking (this is the way he used to wake me up for school when I was little). In the dream, I woke up and heard my grandfather say "let it go."

The next morning I called my dad back in tears and apologized to him. I forgave him for not being there for me and I told him until I could reconcile my feelings for him I would never be good for my husband or any other man. Since I was crying so much, he thought something had happened to me overnight. However, the apology was really more for me than him. Even if he didn't understand it, it was the medicine I needed for my soul. It was my first step to freedom.

Not long after that conversation, my church's Women's Ministry had an event and we were asked to place things in a basket that we wanted to get rid of. I put "fear of abandonment" there but still didn't completely let it go. A month or so later as my marriage seemed destined for failure, I was feeling powerless. This time nothing that I seemed to do was "right" in my husband's mind. I decided it was time to stop trying to please him and deal with me. The time had come for me to rid myself of the baggage I had carried for way too long. I was worn out from working so hard trying to be the best at everything. I decided that the fear of being left alone had to leave my life. It was killing me.

I realized I had been trying all my life to prove to those people who were important to me, that I was worthy so they wouldn't leave me. It had to stop. This resulted in me moving out of our house and really beginning to confront my greatest fear. I decided that the fear of being alone would no longer control me. That fear had allowed me to accept anything from anybody and it was coming to an end. I had to find out why I was so afraid of being alone. I had to break free.

Guess what? I learned I had nothing to fear. While the journey has not been without some bumps, getting to know *me* has been invaluable. God is constantly working on my spirit through messages and people I come in contact with. Most importantly, it is the silence around me that has done the most for me. It has caused me to look inside and recognize that I had the power all along to love myself and be comfortable being alone. In fact, being alone is not at all what I feared it would be. Finally facing it has made all the difference in my outlook.

I learned that I don't have to do anything but be myself and the world will have to accept me on those terms and not the other way around. Not long ago my dad was in town and we got to share some special moments. He was upset about my marital situation and as we talked about it, he saw me break down and cry uncontrollably. Then a tender moment occurred – one that I had longed for all my life. My dad responded with a simple hug and told me "What's done is done. Now move on." That's never happened in all of my 44 years and it was liberating. I've accepted that my marriage is over and I've filed for divorce. I have accepted the past and realize that I cannot rewrite history with my dad. I've emerged from my storm stronger, more confident and **most importantly,** free in more ways than one. I can only thank God.

"Rising From Ashes" – Yvonne's Story

On July 19, 1989, my husband, Lemm Allen Sr., was a passenger aboard United Airlines flight # 232. Once in flight, the plane, destined for Chicago, Illinois, experienced hydraulic failure and crashed into a cornfield outside of Sioux City, Iowa. Due to the heroic maneuvers of United Airlines pilot, Al Haynes, 285 passengers and 10 crew members managed to survive. This tragic incident earned Flight # 232 a place in aviation history. It was the first commercial airline catastrophe to have more survivors than fatalities. My husband, however, was listed among the 111 passengers and 1 crew member who perished. That day a part of me died too.

The fear of having to face all of the responsibility for my family emotionally and financially was too much. I nearly destroyed what was left of our family, because I could not step forward and be the strong "head of the family" that my children, Karla then 19 and Lemm Jr., 17 needed and were accustomed to having. Lemm Sr. had been that figure in our home and now he was gone. I had lost my husband and soulmate. My children had lost their father and they almost lost me too.

On the day after the crash, I remember telling them that my life was over and I had nothing to give them. Fear stripped me of the confidence I needed to accept the sudden new role as head of the household. My children were young with wonderful futures ahead of them. My fears were standing in the way of doing what I needed to do to support them emotionally.

I was so angry with God for taking Lemm, and angry with Lemm for dying when so many had lived. I even resented my kids and everyone else who cared about me. I wanted to be left alone to wallow in a self-imposed prison of despair and isolation. All of my family and friends came to comfort and support me. My girlfriends, relatives and close friends flew in from all over the country. I did not have to lift a finger or make a decision. Well-intentioned loved ones managed everything. However, no one, not even me, gave my two children the emotional support they deserved. Everyone's focus was on me.

My children suffered because I was not emotionally there for them when they needed me most. Instead of dealing with my children, I dealt with the deeds. There were times after the internment that I was annoyed when my children attempted to schedule some special time with me. Couldn't they see that I was busy with the estate and trying to make us financially secure? I kept pushing them away. I was wrong. Suddenly, like the sun coming out from behind the clouds after a torrential rain, it dawned on me that I could either climb into that crypt with Lemm and hide from life or I could accept life's new challenges by acknowledging and proving I was strong enough to care for myself and my family.

God helped me to face that fear. Through His infinite wisdom, God knew I had the capacity and knowledge to accomplish what was necessary to keep my family together and establish myself as a competent independent woman. He gave me the confidence that I lacked to take care of things. My role was simply to let God reveal to me why there was no need to fear; that things could get resolved and I could go on.

That was the turning point. I emerged from the ashes of United 232's crash. The old cliché, "Time Heals All Wounds", is a greatly exaggerated myth to me. I believe time allows us to learn simply how to adjust and live successfully within the realm of life's challenges and changes. It gives us the opportunity to adjust to our circumstances, fill the void and move on with life.

In retrospect, I now accept responsibility for the mistakes I initially made concerning my children. Fortunately, they are now adults raising their own children. Karla and Lemm don't need a parent now the way a child does so we have become friends who enjoy spending holidays and quality time together. Each of us still misses Lemm, Sr. and had to travel different roads to acquire the strength to adjust to his loss. However, the most important thing is that the three of us are a family who love and appreciate each other for who we are.

The family unit has expanded to include my new husband, Luther. We married in 2000 and now reside in Charlotte, North Carolina, where Luther and my stepdaughter own and manage a restaurant. I now have three grandchildren — Aniyah, Julian and Giselle, who are worthy of another story. They are the light of my life.

The strength I gained from this experience is priceless. By staring fear in the face, acknowledging and accepting what it cost me and moving on, I am a better person. In spite of my past parental failures, both my children grew up to be healthy productive adults and somewhere along the way I grew up too.

"But God" – Jackie's Story

I spent most of my childhood and a good portion of my adult-life trying to find the love I had lost when my father left home. My father and I had always had a strained relationship and I realize now that he was battling his own demons. Most of the time he avoided me and I thought it was because he didn't love me or that I was unworthy. This made me determined to prove myself worthy in every way. I had no problems succeeding in most areas of my life, but when it came to men, I could never seem to make a relationship work. In retrospect, I realize that I was too needy.

At seventeen, I married and thought my quest for love had ended. Initially, my husband and I enjoyed living life in the fast lane. However, two years into the marriage, my husband accepted his call to preach the Gospel. I had been raised to believe in God and attended church regularly, but I didn't have a personal experience with Him. My husband and I were married for ten years and had three children. He was a good provider and devoted to his family.

In August 1998, I decided we should separate because I felt there was no excitement in the relationship. Romance novels and storybooks told me that there were things that I should be experiencing in my marriage that I wasn't. I couldn't appreciate the fact that above all, this man was devoted to God. My decision to seek happiness outside of the church negatively impacted everyone and not long after that, my husband stepped down from the ministry.

In seeking all the excitement that the romance novels said I should have, I soon found myself in a new relationship. This one came with excitement, but it also came with more drama and pain than I could ever imagine. For the next three years, I would remain in a turbulent relationship in which I had invested everything trying to make it work. It was the devil's plan to use this man to destroy me. But God promised in Jeremiah 29:11 "For I know the plans I have for you," … "plans to prosper you and not to harm you, plans to give you hope and a future."

I realize now that this man had become my idol and it was unimaginable to me that I could exist without him in my life. My self-worth was so low. I knew this relationship was destroying both me and my relationship with my family and friends. At the time, I was unwilling to fail at another relationship so I kept trying. I believed that if I could just get someone to love me, I would no longer have to fill a void. Unfortunately, this person was just as needy as me and two incomplete people cannot make a healthy relationship.

One day, I realized I was on the verge of losing my sanity and financial stability. My friends felt they could no longer help me. My health started to decline from worry and self-neglect. I was hurting and started to drink to numb my pain. I had always been a drinker, but only in a crisis. Once the crisis was over, I would put the bottle away until the next time. But this time was different; my consumption was steadily increasing. What started out as one or two drinks in the evening soon became half a bottle. Before long, the half a bottle became a fifth a day. My magic cure was no longer working.

I continued to attend church and hold together the facade of having everything in order. But, I was sinking and felt there was no way out. I started to question whether or not God existed. My children couldn't believe that I was questioning the very thing that I taught them to believe in. My children and my ex-husband prayed for me and sought the Lord when I would not seek Him for myself.

I wrestled with ending my current relationship and ultimately settled on a 90-day separation. Immediately, I began to question my decision because the fear of not being loved had controlled me for most of my life. When the fears began to overwhelm me, I didn't know what to do with myself. While lying in my bed, I cried out to God in the name of Jesus to save me. Immediately God took away the desire to hide from my pain through alcohol. The path following that hasn't been easy. I had many sleepless nights and tears but God saw me through. It was during my lowest point that I felt and came to know the joy of the Lord. He helped me conquer my fears and realize that through every situation, He had been with me.

Finally, I found the love I had spent a lifetime trying to earn in God. Through the years, I had allowed the devil to emphasize all my mistakes. Now, I know I can count on God. His grace has been sufficient to help me overcome fear and to appreciate the pain I've experienced. What the devil meant to use to destroy me, God used to shape me. There is no other explanation that I will accept.

Lessons Learned

- Fear is not of God but is learned.

- Fear stops us from being all that we can be.

Exercise for the Day

1. Write down three things that you fear most.
2. Write down - If I didn't fear _____ I could do
_____. The goal is to see how eliminating your fear of
something elevates you to do more.
3. Recite the following prayer:

*God you have not given me a spirit of fear. You give me
power. I take back my power over (**item that you fear**).
Today I choose to be free and to know the truth.
Create in me a spirit of boldness and confidence to
go forward and be all that you would have me be.*

CHAPTER 3

CONCEPTUALIZE A SOLUTION

"Visualize this thing you want. See it, feel it, believe in it.
Make your mental blueprint and begin."
Robert Collier

Many of us have heard "If you don't know where you're going, any road will get you there." Without a roadmap, guide or point of reference, it is difficult to get anything done. Knowing what you want, its purpose and the potential outcome are essential to making a change in your life or navigating through rough passages.

If needing to know where we're going is so important, why do so many of us ignore or simply fail to create a vision for ourselves? Why would something that important be left to chance or to someone else? Our vision, much like our fingerprint, is unique. It captures our thoughts, dreams, aspirations and those things that are important to us. Having some definitive purpose and a way to communicate it to yourself and others around you, help to set boundaries. It allows you to evaluate what you will and will not do.

According to the late Harvard Business professor, Theodore Levitt, "The future belongs to those who see possibilities before they become obvious." Who better to see the possibilities for us than we ourselves? What's the process for getting there? While the process for creating personal vision may be as unique as the vision itself, there are some common tools that we can use – silence, prayer and personal inventory. The power of silence can be used to shape our vision. Ilyana Vanzant advocates the positive use of silence "to listen, hear and feel." According to Vanzant, once we learn how to use silence we are better able "to translate into words what you are feeling."

The integration of specific prayer on our purpose cannot be understated. Desiring to please God should motivate us to seek His guidance in creating a vision that moves us towards achieving more with our gifts and talents. Our greatest role model in knowing and accepting our purpose is Jesus. Max Lucado reminds us that, "Jesus refused to be guided by anything other than His high call." If we seek God in prayer to understand our purpose, we can make it our goal. Knowing we have consulted God and are obedient to His direction, can elevate our confidence.

Finally, conducting personal inventory helps to shape our vision. Personal inventory simply refers to "taking stock" in what makes you special. Ann Roulac, author of Power, Passion and Purpose: 7 Steps to Energizing Your Life," suggests that you "tap into your own power center." The power center represents your inner voice. What things are you good at? What things are you not so good at? What do you like to do? What would you like to do that you aren't doing now? What does your personal happiness look like for you? What are you missing (e.g., skills, experiences, contacts, education, etc.)? This requires you to be honest with yourself. It also demands that you be creative and open to **new** ideas – not more of the same. Remember the purpose of this inventory is to help you focus and give you direction - so don't limit yourself.

Paul and Sarah Edwards in their book Changing Directions Without Losing Your Way have provided a great framework that can be used to gain clarity and create personal vision. They use the "R" concept (another powerful play on words) – Retreat (get outside your status quo), Rest (you need energy and enthusiasm to think creatively), Relax (connect with the inner you), and Reflect (where you've been, where you are and where you are going). This personal inventory exercise will help to craft a vision that is more closely aligned with your uniqueness. The intent is to develop a vision that will make **you** and **only you** happy. With your personal blueprint created; your mental map established; and your confidence and self-knowledge in tact, you can get to work in reshaping and redefining yourself.

"If There's a Way Out – I'm Taking It" – Traci's Story

Senior year in high school brings about so many questions in most students' minds. Some of the common things that are important are:

- "What dress am I going to wear to prom?"
- "What am I going to do after high school?"
- "Will I be able to afford to go to college?"
- "Will I score high enough on the SAT?"

While I thought about those things too, there were other pressing issues in my household. Each day when I came home from school, my primary concerns were basic human needs and my parents' frame of mind. Would we have lights? Would we have food for dinner? My senior year was full of constant turmoil at my house and my family faced much uncertainty and instability at a time when I needed it most.

Initially, we led a relatively normal life. My mom, dad, younger siblings and I lived together in a nice home with a lot of amenities. I was a child then and didn't notice that things were steadily changing and becoming more chaotic. My family and home life began to crumble and since we lived in a small town, I thought everyone knew it. I felt shame and was embarrassed but what could I do? I spent a lot of time with my grandparents trying to escape the turmoil at home, which bought about my biggest guilt: leaving my younger siblings in an uneasy situation. I often had to be the parents for them when our parents just couldn't be.

The situation was sometimes overwhelming to me and I kept asking "Why me?" I simply did not understand why I had to deal with this. I felt like I was leading a double life – "picture perfect" girl to the outside world and yet full of turmoil on the inside. It would have been easy to take the path of least resistance during this time. I could have just resolved that my life was bad and would stay that way. I could have just given up any hope of going to college. Perhaps, I could have become pregnant and a teenage mother. Given everything going on around me, I could have turned to drugs and alcohol or just checked out mentally. Despite this, I had an inner resolve that my situation was not going to get the best of me.

Even though my home life was getting worse daily, I still felt that my parents, extended family and teachers wanted me to be successful and this kept me motivated. I constantly visualized a life outside of my current situation and outside of North Carolina. I knew with my grades and extracurricular activities I had a shot at something different. I had plans to succeed somehow despite my environment.

During a college visit to Georgetown University, I met an admissions officer whose hometown was less than 30 miles from mine. Her encouragement was a turning point for me. After that chance meeting, I believed that I could successfully get into Georgetown and visualized myself on the campus. I believed it could make a difference in my life. Georgetown was my "light at the end of the tunnel." I only applied to two schools – Georgetown and a state school (just as a backup). I realized that in order to survive, I had to see things outside of my current situation. I needed a significant change away from vices, addictions, and family responsibilities. Going to school in North Carolina could not and would not provide that.

From a cost perspective Georgetown was clearly more expensive than a North Carolina state school. However, I could still envision myself on Georgetown's campus and knew I would be able to attend with God's help. God did not let me down. Not only did I get into Georgetown, but the financial aid package was more than I could have hoped for. Georgetown opened my eyes to another world. There were so many possibilities. I was not going to be a victim, but a victor and this educational opportunity helped me accomplish that.

It has taken me some time to reconcile the feelings I had while going through that storm in my life. However, as I look back now, I'm at peace with those years because it helped to make me who I am today. God purposed my path and it helped me to grow and create a better life for my family and I. Without a vision of a better life as a constant blueprint, I don't know how this would have been accomplished. The odds were stacked against me and giving up would have been a lot easier. I refused to give in; I had a vision. I had a goal and when God made a way, I took it.

"But I Have a Friend in Need" - Janice's Story

Knowing your purpose in life has its advantages. I always knew I wanted to be an advocate for the needy. Fortunately, I have been able to work with various organizations that provide these services. In my hometown of Omaha, I worked for Women Infants and Children (WIC), one of the largest social service programs in Nebraska. This position allowed me to start an inner city WIC program that eventually became the largest program in Omaha.

I relocated to Virginia and began working for a non-profit, faith-based organization that provided food, shelter and clothing services to the needy. Being of service to others was my job and pleasure. People would frequently stop me at church, in the grocery store or basically anywhere they saw me to share a problem, tell of someone in need, or just to pray for my mission. The need was great. I was able to arrange for my office building to be turned into a winter warming center so men, women and children would have a place to go to stay warm. Being able to organize this brought me joy.

However, a management change threatened to move me away from what I knew I was supposed to be doing. It challenged me to be very clear about whom I am and my purpose. From the beginning, I felt the new executive director did not like me. She told me, "I hear you are good at fundraising. I know that I am good and you will take direction from me." I was assigned tasks that were precise and time consuming. I was instructed to eliminate my interaction with the homeless. My role was to be a fundraiser and not a friend to the homeless. What a dilemma – pursuing purpose vs. meeting the bills. After prayer and consultation with a former executive director, I decided to resign. His advice was "Don't worry about tomorrow, about what you will wear or what you will eat." Sound familiar?

My resignation was submitted and I was told to leave the premises immediately. As painful as that was, I did as instructed. I knew God would not forsake me. The very next day, I received a call from the minister who originally started the non-profit that I had just resigned from. We met and worked on a vision for a project that brought me back to the work that was more closely related to my purpose.

That led to a collaborative effort of clergy, individuals and corporations resulting in the birth of Circle of Love Coalition, Inc. I feel good knowing that I will continue helping those in need. There is a quote from Jawaharlal Nehru that says, "Life is like a game of cards. The hand that is dealt you represents determinism; the way you play it is free will." Knowing my purpose and vision and letting others know about it helped me to create a venue to continue doing more of what I love to do. It doesn't get any better than that.

"If I Can Just Get Free" – Peggy's Story

By the age of 15, I had already had a son out of wedlock. When I was 17 my mother told me that there were too many adults in the house so I had to move. Prior to graduating from high school, I worked and lived in subsidized housing. One day I met a guy who needed a battery jump. I helped him and we began what would be a long and abusive relationship. I confused love with lust and we were married before I graduated from high school. We relocated to Germany because my husband received military orders. After moving, the abuse became so bad, I actually plotted to kill him. I felt I could do it and no one would suspect me. I was raised in a Christian home and knew this was not right. I prayed and asked God to take the thought away from me. I promised God that if He would get me safely back to the United States, I would give my life to Him. He kept His promise, but I didn't keep mine.

Once back in the US, I divorced my husband. Instead of keeping my promise to God, I got back in the fast lane and fell in love with another man. If he said, "Jump!" I would say, "How high?" Everything was fine at first and I thought this relationship was going to be better.

When he went away to prison, I visited him every week. Once he came home things started to get bad. He was abusive but I thought we were "in love" so I let things slide that I shouldn't have. He was very popular around town – complete with money, fancy cars, and of course *women*. Things got so bad that my mother warned me to get away from him before he killed me. I left town to stay with my sister for a while. Of course he called and begged me to come back. He promised that things would be different. I came back, but it wasn't long before things were back to "normal."

The breaking point for me was when I came home from a hospital visit and found him lying in the bed with another woman. I told him I was leaving him and he snapped. The next thing I knew he put a double-barreled shotgun in my mouth and held a machete to my neck. There was a friend in the house who helped me get away from him. He opened the door and told me to run. I ran and hid in a ditch because I knew he would come after me. After I heard cars go by and was sure he was gone, I ran to the first house with a light on it to ask for help. I was a mess and the people drove me to the Sheriff's Office where I took out a warrant on him.

He begged me not to press charges against him and I agreed but I left town and stayed with family. I believed it was the only way to save myself. I could not see myself living that life anymore. I knew there was something else I was purposed for but I needed to be free. A strange bus ride back home to visit my son gave me the courage to move on. When I boarded the bus, there was only one empty seat. When I sat down, I shared a conversation with a man. He showed me a plane ticket for a flight to our destination that he was scheduled to take. Instead, he said God told him to take the bus. This didn't seem like a chance encounter. He told me that I needed to make a choice and that I should stay where I was. God would make a way for me.

When I got back in town, my boyfriend found out I was there and he sent a driver for me. When I said, "no I wasn't going", he came himself to get me. When I told him I wasn't going with him anymore, that was a defining moment for me. He left the house and told me to "Let my God take care of me then."

I returned back to where I was living, did exceptionally well on my job and met someone new. This time I had a different approach – build a friendship first. My new friend and I talked on the phone, never dated and had no sex; I asked *him* to marry *me*.

I never forgot what the man on the bus told me. I began to think about God's plan for my life and what I could see myself doing. I wanted to own a business. My current job kept me traveling for long periods of time. My new husband asked me to choose my career or my family. I began to pray. I asked God to give me something to do that would allow me to give Him honor and lend support to my family. God had bought me through so much and I needed His guidance on my business venture.

From the time I was a little girl, I always loved things clean, neat and in order. I decided to start a cleaning service. I opened my business while I was still employed. My first contract was with a Radio Shack store. The store manager said if I could make his floors look white he would give me all the stores in the area. I made his floors white and have not looked back since. Within two years, my company's revenue was over $2.5 million and I am still in the business today.

My vision for myself was love not abuse. I knew that there was something else I was destined for. I just needed to be free and gain the confidence to move forward. Once I was freed from the abusive relationship, God placed all the right people and opportunities in front of me. I made growing my business my goal and with hard work and determination it has worked out for me. I don't reflect on the past. My vision keeps me looking forward and it feels good.

Lessons Learned

- Our vision is our unique blueprint for our life – we own the creation, management and execution of it.

- Negative experiences and people will enter our lives but they must never hinder us from achieving our vision.

Exercise for the Day

1. Take the time to follow the recommendations in the chapter – get silent (listen to the inner you); pray to God for His guidance on your purpose; conduct your personal inventory.
2. Be prepared to answer the following questions:
    a. I am _____.
    b. I can do _____ well.
    c. I will use my talents in _____ to the highest and best use to achieve my purpose.
3. Write your vision out. Make it incorporate the work you've done in #1 and #2 above. Writing it down helps you to describe it, see it and then own it.
4. Recite the following prayer:

God you have told us that every good and perfect gift comes from you. Lord, I want to use my gifts for greater service to you. Please help me to identify and understand my gifts and give me clarity and a vision for my life.

CHAPTER 4

CREATE A PLAN

"Action may not always bring happiness,
but there is no happiness without action."
Benjamin Disraeli

There's an old adage that says, "Failure to Plan is Planning to Fail." Once we have a vision or purpose, the next step is to create a plan to ensure its fulfillment. The plan becomes the roadmap for achieving specific goals. While some may think a plan is reserved for businesses, athletic teams or the like, the reality is living without a plan hinders us from reaching our full potential. We must be willing to determine the necessary steps to obtain our goals.

We are often faced with situations that require action. How we respond or not respond may heavily depend upon our own internal plan. Therefore we need a benchmark or a barometer to evaluate potential courses of action. Drs. Kirschner and Brinkman in their book <u>Life by Design: Making Wise Choices in a Mixed-Up World</u> suggests that plans "do not allow us to control reality, they do allow us to take action, to move forward, to bring pieces of our goals to life, and along the way, to learn that we are surrounded by resources available for our use and advantages waiting to be taken for our benefit."

For some of you, your goal may be to lose weight, purchase your first home, get out of debt, send a child to college or go back to school. Whatever your personal goal, I consider the following factors to be the most important as you plan:

1. Write it Down. This is your way of communicating to yourself what you want. Henriette Klauser suggests in her book <u>Write It Down, Make It Happen: Knowing What You Want and Getting It</u> that "It is up to you to trust the possibility enough to be willing to put your dream in writing, and to take the first step, even with no evidence that it will actually happen."

2. Put a Timeline Around It. This keeps you accountable to yourself - Set a date and work towards it (I will complete this by…). This helps to prevent procrastination. The timeline forces you to think about what you need and are able to accomplish within a specific timeframe. It also helps you to track your progress. Ask yourself, "How well am I doing?" "Are there resources that I need in order to be successful?" "What roadblocks may hinder me from making my date?"

3. Prioritize. As you begin constructing your plan, you will find that everything cannot be accomplished all at once. Therefore, identify what is most important and prioritize accordingly. This will keep you focused. This effort isn't an attempt to "eat an entire elephant," but rather a guide to help you set meaningful goals for your lives. The plan is not intended to be rigid. It is a living document, always available for tailoring as your needs or goals change. So why not plan? Create your own recipe for living. The world is waiting to respond to those who are clear about their direction and purpose.

Whatever your personal goal is – just don't forget to plan.

"What God Has For Me" – Angel's story (alias used)

I was married for 11 years to a man who cheated on me. I thought I had a great life — a beautiful home, career and three lovely girls. Nothing was good enough for my husband. Not only did he cheat on me with other women, but he also had another child outside of our marriage. I tried to forgive him but when he wouldn't stop cheating, I left him. I later married another man and converted to Islam. I thought things would be better. I was tired of being alone. He was very nice but there were things I didn't know about him prior to getting married. The marriage was a disaster. I divorced him and became frustrated at everything – including my surroundings.

I convinced a friend to relocate with me across several states to an area I thought would be more open to Muslims. While my family didn't understand, my mother did support me. I was a single mother struggling to raise three children. I wasn't making a lot of money at the time. I had terrible credit as a result of my second marriage and I thought I could never own a home on my own. In spite of my circumstances, I needed to prove to myself I could do this. One of my daughter's friend's mom, was a realtor and she told me about a special program that would allow me to purchase a home. She helped me create a plan. The loan processor told me in order to qualify for the loan, I would have to clean up my credit and pay off over $2,000 worth of outstanding debt. This amount was in addition to the closing costs associated with the loan. The money needed for debt payoff, down payment and closing was greater than I could earn at one job. At the time, I only made $11 an hour. Fortunately, I had time on my side since. The county program applied to new construction homes and I had time during construction to get my money together. I took on two more jobs and instead of working a 12- hour shift I sometimes worked 24 hours straight – not going home.

I realized that I couldn't pay the rent for my apartment and get the money together I needed to buy the new home. However, God placed people in my life to help me in this situation. First my friend that moved with me to the new state let me stay with her rent- free while the home was being built. Another family took in my children and cared for them as if they were their own. My children stayed with this family for over six months while the home was being built.

I was exhausted from working so much. Every time I got paid from a job I would keep just enough out to have gas and transportation and I would either pay off a debt or take money to the builder. I would go by the house every day and pray to God to help me get through to own my own home. The loan was approved but as the closing drew closer, I still needed additional money for the closing. My realtor helped me apply for a county loan that would give me enough money for settlement. There wasn't a dry eye in the room when the keys were handed to me.

I was able to put a plan together, work the plan (even though all those jobs nearly killed me) and the result for me was a home without the help of a spouse. I was so proud of myself for that. Sometimes as women we don't realize the strength God provides until we find ourselves in a situation where we have to use it. You can work through anything with a plan. God puts people in your life to tell you He's got a blessing for you. You've got to receive it and act on your plan. What God had for me was for me and I thank Him for it.

"The Best Plan I Can Think Of" – Marjorie's Story

I'd been struggling with lumps in my breast for years. Every time I would find a lump, I would to go to the doctor for a checkup. They would drain the lump and test it. The results always came back negative and I'd move on. I was totally devastated and unprepared for the big "C" diagnosis, as both my grandparents had died from cancer.

The exact timing of my diagnosis was critical. I had recently relocated from North Carolina to Florida and was working a job without benefits. The secretary in the department was very concerned that I didn't have benefits. She told me about an available position that included benefits and encouraged me to apply. I was a little concerned because other candidates had already applied. Nevertheless, I applied for the job and got it without the other candidates being interviewed. I hadn't thought about benefits any more until the insurance cards arrived. I made an appointment with the doctor for a checkup. I explained my history to the doctor and while he was feeling a new lump in my breast, he thought it was probably more of the same. He did, however, refer me to a surgeon who did a needle biopsy. The results came back positive.

I listened to the doctor but I don't remember what he said about my condition or treatment. I didn't ask any questions. I just went to see the oncologist, and completed all the scans and tests that he ordered. I wasn't able to explain my treatment plan to my sister-in-law so she flew down to Florida to accompany me to my appointments. I had to come up with a "plan of attack". My plan centered around one theme – knowing that God was my all and that Jesus Christ was the center of my life. The one thing that I believed, despite what the doctors were saying, is the Word of God.

I wasn't handling my situation well and was having problems maintaining my sanity. So, I decided to put my trust in God. God knows best and is in charge of the outcome. I believed my day was already set in Heaven and there was nothing I could do to change it. Therefore, I needed to know that I would be with Jesus throughout eternity and I resolved to live the rest of my life on earth to please the Lord.

Two scriptures remained in my spirit during this time – Hebrews 9:27 "Just as man is destined to die once, and after that to face judgment"; and Philippians 1:21 "For me to live is Christ and to die is to gain." I knew that God loved me so much and no matter what life brought to me, I would be cared for. At that point, I was at peace with whatever the outcome.

God did care for me during this period, especially during the worst part of the treatment, chemotherapy. I had not worked long enough to accumulate leave so God allowed two things to happen. First, He made it possible for me to work in the office instead of the field. This was a blessing because the heat and elements worked against my treatment. Second, He made it possible for me to work Monday through Friday. This enabled me to take chemotherapy on the weekends. When I had bouts with nausea, God comforted me. Further, after the surgery, I was never in pain. In fact, my sister-in-law immediately filled the prescription I received from the hospital, but I never had to use it! When I went through radiation, I would leave treatment and go back to work feeling fine.

I have learned that Romans 8:28 is true "And we know that in all things God works for the good of those who love him, who have been called according to his purpose." We look at things with our natural eyes but things are never as they seem. We hardly ever see what God is trying to do to perfect our lives for His purpose. We were created for His purpose. In the midst of a serious health concern, I put my life "in the hands of a Man who hadn't lost a case." His plan became my plan and I am here today to tell others about His grace.

"Eating to Live" – Sandy's Story

I've had a big change of lifestyle and size! I've gone from squeezing into a size 26 to an average size 4. A change in my diet, the way I feel about food and love for myself has made all the difference. My thoughts about food and myself were both negatively impacted during early childhood. As a young child, I always felt I didn't have enough to eat. My mother had divorced when I was young and we relocated from New York to South Carolina. However, my mother struggled to work and raise four children. We often went without breakfast and in general, food was limited in our home. A visit to my grandmother's house was like a big visit to the grocery store. I never wanted to leave there. Food was plentiful and packed with sugar and carbohydrates such as breads. I consumed it all.

When I was 8 years old, a family member molested me. This terrible experience took away my innocence and tainted the way I felt about the opposite sex and myself. I thought food was the one thing that I could control. The truth is it began to control me. I was thin until I got married. During my first pregnancy, I ate for two and gained 96 pounds. After the baby arrived, I had problems losing the weight so I just kept overeating to hide my pain.

My ex-husband was abusive, mentally, emotionally and physically which kept my self-esteem very low. As I gained weight, he would call me names and I began to believe all the horrible things he said about me. This led to more unhealthy food consumption and weight gain. I didn't want any attention from the opposite sex.

I would binge eat on all types of fast foods but my favorite was triple cheeseburgers and fries. In addition to the heavy fast food diet, every day I would cook and eat full course meals. Saturday's meals included huge breakfasts of ham, bacon, French toast, grits and more. I guess I was making up for the lack of breakfast during my childhood. I would eat it all. The more I ate, the less I exercised. I had been very athletic in high school and had to maintain an exercise regiment while in the military. I knew I had the ability to exercise and kept saying I could lose weight, but never made the effort to do so. Instead, I continued to eat excessively and pack on the pounds. Food was my comforter when I was lonely or depressed. It became a personal reward when I had accomplished something big.

I couldn't believe how much weight I had gained and that began to affect me. On a visit to my hometown, my old physical education teacher remarked that they couldn't believe how fat I had become. I was the high school queen in 1982 and had now ballooned to 240 pounds. I wanted to do something about it but really didn't have the tools to be successful at that time. I had previously tried many diets including the Beverly Hills Diet, Atkins, Weight Watchers, Jennie Craig and more. I would go on fitness regiments I learned in the military and would sculpt the perfect body. Unfortunately within a few weeks or months, I started back with the fast food. I would put cheese and ketchup on everything. My biggest weaknesses were bread, my grandmother's cakes, Aunt Ruth's Lemon Meringue pie, homemade biscuits, flaky piecrusts, homemade cookies, and homemade bread that had be to drenched in butter and lots of dill weed. Any weight that I was able to lose quickly returned.

My liberation day was February 6, 2006. A friend introduced me to a holistic doctor that would change and save my life. He gave me a plan to regain my health and self esteem. The plan was rigid, but it helped me lose weight and feel good. It included education, discipline, herbal vitamins and supplements and eliminating foods such as: vinegar, sweeteners/honey/sugar, fruit juices, dried fruits, grapes & raisins, coffee, wheat/corn, yeast, wine/beer, cheese/milk, carbonated drinks, fried foods, and ice cold drinks. The plan also included fish oil to keep my heart pumping and my skin tight during the weight loss. By the fall of that year, I had lost 140 pounds! I have two more phases to complete and I will be done. Maintenance is very low.

If I eat something on the list by mistake, I usually cleanse that night with a colon cleanser.

Understanding how the body works and how food affects it was beneficial to me. Knowing what foods to avoid helped me successfully meet my weight loss goals. Where I used to eat a pint of butter pecan Haagen Dazs ice cream at night, I now eat 3 to 4 red grapefruit as a midnight snack. I eat lots of nuts and I find now that my system craves what it is lacking. I eat cashews by the pound. I eat Fuji apples, strawberries, navel oranges, watermelon, cantaloupe and honeydew melons. I can have any kind of meat I want but I stay away from beef because it takes about five days to digest. In order to stay on my plan, I have created a variety of dishes with meats and vegetables. When eating out, I usually ask the wait staff to explain my diet to the chef and come up with some creative dishes as well.

My confidence is higher and I feel better about everything. The investment in the herbal supplements recommended by the doctor was a wise investment. I am pleased beyond words with the results. I now know that food is not a cure for depression or loneliness and I don't need an excuse to eat. A solid plan and personal discipline put me on the right track. Instead of living to eat, I now eat to live and it feels great!

Lessons Learned

- Living without a plan limits our ability to reach our full potential.

- Commit to writing down a plan. Hold yourself accountable to complete it and prioritizing the most important items to complete.

Exercise for the Day

1. As you review your vision and purpose document from the previous chapter, begin to write down how you intend to accomplish the vision. What do you need? When can you get it done? What's most important?
2. Create reminders and affirmations to yourself that will motivate you to keep going on your plan.
3. Recite the following prayer :

Lord you have told us in Your Word that "the race is not given to the swift nor the battle to the strong... but time and chance happen to them all (Ecclesiastes 9:11)" Now is my time to take advantage of all that You have for me. I pray that You will give me wisdom and guidance to construct a plan for my life. I want to glorify You by living my life abundantly and to my full potential. Give me the strength and I will plan instead of failing to plan.

CHAPTER 5

COMMIT TO MAKING IT HAPPEN

"First say to yourself what you would be;
and then do what you have to do."
Epictetus

Once your vision is established, and your plan created, the next step is to identify what you need to be successful and act upon it. Ask yourself - Are there people I need to get support from? Is there a course I need to take to advance my goal? What dedicated time do I need to get it done? What do I need to remain motivated to get the task done? This effort requires you to be clear about what you need to make your plan successful and go after it with dedication and determination.

Regardless of the task required, you must have an unwavering commitment to see your plan through.

You must be the number one person to get the job done. As a caution, choose to share your plan only with positive influences. Sometimes people who don't understand what you're trying to do or who are in a different place than you, can pull you off course. If you can do this, moving forward becomes less challenging.

Ilyana Vanzant says in her book <u>Yesterday I Cried</u> – "when you make up your mind to take a stand, forces from out of nowhere will appear to support you."

Your commitment will be evident to everyone around you and the support that will come your way will be overwhelming. The book <u>Jesus CEO: Using Ancient Wisdom for Visionary Leadership</u> suggests that we follow the model of Jesus in having "a passionate commitment to the cause." The book further suggests that if you demonstrate passionate commitment, this will be your signal to everyone around you to "make way for someone who knows what he or she wants."

"We're in This Together" – Tommi's Story

My mother has Alzheimer's disease and I am her primary caregiver. I have a full-time job and still maintain responsibility for her care. It didn't start out that way but gradually it became my role. In 1988, my father passed away and while Mom continued to work for a while, her focus began to change. There were many subtle changes that went unnoticed. While my mother's father and sister both suffered from Alzheimer's disease, it didn't dawn on me that Mom might have this disease when she began to repeat herself and forget where she put things.

At first it started with just dementia. She was mobile and able to get around. Later, at an Adult Day Care Center, she was knocked down and suffered a hip fracture that led to hip replacement surgery. Following the surgery, Mom was sent to a rehabilitation center and subsequently a group home for several months. The goal was to get her back on her feet and mobile again. I wasn't comfortable with this arrangement and went every day after work to walk her and get her to bed. My daily presence didn't seem to make a difference in the level of care she received, nor did it aid in Mom's recovery. Despite the dementia, I think she knew she was in a home and it negatively affected her recovery. She was traumatized!

I was not at all satisfied with the care she was receiving and I needed another way. My mother is my very best friend. Now that she was in need, leaving her in a home was just not an option for me. I made a conscious decision to bring her home with me. I had to get a system together that would allow me to work and provide quality level care for her. I remodeled my basement to include a bedroom suite for her so that she could be comfortable and cared for on one level. Next, I had a chairlift installed to allow us to bring her upstairs from time to time to get some sun on her face. My mother isn't able to walk on her own. Even using her walker she can only walk a few steps. I have a caregiver come to the home for twelve hours per day during the week so I can work.

At times I get fatigued caring for Mom. Yet, I feel blessed to still feel her presence, regardless of her condition. She is no longer able to communicate with me, although she tries from time to time. I have accepted her illness and have made the adjustments in my life and home to handle it. With God's strength, we are walking this walk together. I realize providing care for Mom is a huge undertaking, but I am totally committed to it. It required preparation, adjustment and prioritization to make it happen. What I've learned from this is that the little day-to-day annoyances that at one time seemed monumental are just that – annoyances. I now focus on what is really important. My mother, my best friend is in need and I'm glad that I can say "I've got her back."

"A Second Chance" – Dorothy's Story

On January 29, 1989, I had a massive heart attack when I was only 42 years old. At that time, I wasn't saved. I attended church sometimes, smoked cigarettes and did my share of partying. That day started like any other but the circumstances surrounding the events were nothing short of a miracle from God. It would be nearly three weeks before I was even aware of everything that occurred that day and the subsequent days on my behalf.

I was blessed because I worked at a hospital. My break was at 10:30 and I started feeling like I had heartburn. I went to the pharmacy to buy heartburn medicine and a pack of cigarettes. By the time I returned to the break room, I was sweating. The next thing I remember, I was in the Intensive Care Unit for about a week. During that time, my doctor stayed by my bedside. One of the nurses said that she had been working with the doctor for years and had never seen him sit by a patient's bedside before. To God be the glory! Once I was stabilized, I was moved to a more comprehensive hospital for the second phase of my treatment.

During my stay at the hospital, I learned that there were other patients who had the same type of heart attack and didn't make it. I feel blessed to be here. I believe in the power of prayer. God had His angels encamped around me! Prayers were coming from everywhere. People prayed around my bed and at church. I believe the prayers from my friends and family made my situation better.

Once I returned home I went to my first office visit for follow up care. The doctor said to me "Lady, you're supposed to be pushing up daisies." It was only at that time that I learned the severity of my situation. The doctor told me my heart kept quivering and never stopped. They had to code blue me twice (make my heart stop) to get through the surgery. The doctor said I caused him to go gray prematurely. He believed God was the reason for me being here today and I agree.

I was given a second chance at life and I believed it was for a reason. I made a commitment to change my life for the better. I made a commitment to praise and honor God. I adjusted my lifestyle to make it more pleasing to God. I believe prayer played a big part in my healing, so I have made prayer a part of my life. I turned my life over to Christ, joined a Bible teaching church and am striving to be what I know God wants me to be. I am nicer to people and I don't take anything for granted. Every time I see the two doctors who were on duty that fateful day back in 1989, I thank them. I thank God for this attention-getting experience.

Note: On August 11, 2007 Dorothy passed away suddenly. She was scheduled to be consecrated as a Deaconess in her church on August 26, 2007. Her appointment was conveyed and confirmed posthumously. She will be missed.

"Finally Where I Belong" – Glenda's Story

As long as I can remember, I have been a high achiever. I was programmed early in life to excel and encouraged to handle the hard stuff. By 7th grade I was performing on a 12th grade level and making straight A's. My life changed when I went to work in Corporate America. I found that my managers and co-workers did not see me as a "star performer" and were often intimidated by my performance. I am a confident, capable, and candid African-American woman. If I were a white male, I would probably be leading a Fortune 500 company. But as accomplished as I am, I had to learn a lesson that would finally take me off the corporate treadmill of trying to conform and place me as the CEO of my own firm.

The time it took me to learn this lesson cost me more than I imagined. The stress associated with trying to fit in significantly impacted my health. The years of outstanding reviews that resulted in no promotions took its toll on me and I was diagnosed with kidney failure.

Initially I couldn't understand why this happened to me. My performance was stellar. I consistently exceeded all job requirements and I constantly networked within the organization including participating in corporate recreational/entertainment activities. Regardless of my performance, I wasn't liked any better within the organization. I was constantly responding to feedback from mentors and managers and felt I could fix whatever the organization thought was wrong with me. I took on all of the difficult tasks and excelled, but the organization's response was no promotion. I didn't realize that regardless of performance, once my name was on that list, managers would simply resort to making sure their families were fed first and I became a casualty. I just couldn't be happy in that environment. I wanted and felt I had earned a seat at the table.

I adopted several practices that allowed me to remain within the organization. For other African Americans in Corporate America who may find themselves in similar situations, I offer the following suggestions:

1. Do not isolate yourself in the midst of turmoil. Stay active. Do not whine about your circumstances.
2. Understand your organization including position and the associated compensation levels.
3. Tell people around you about your performance – even if the news isn't great. They will later be able to decipher negative messages because they've heard all types of news directly from you.
4. Keep a journal of your daily activities. This maybe useful to confirm or refute the organization's facts and/or records.
5. Be a strong advocate and supporter of each other. Seek out others and extend yourself to them. You never know when you may need to help each other in a situation.

Finally, I decided that my many years with some of the most respected organizations in the world had indeed earned me a seat at the table – my own. I now am running my own successful business and am focusing on my health. I have identified what I need to be successful and stress free and am fully committed to my lifestyle change. In a recent *O Magazine,* Oprah Winfrey states, "you keep asking the right questions of yourself, and the universe and your own secrets will unfold in ways you never imagined." And as they unfold I continue to thank God for what He is doing for me.

Lessons Learned

- The #1 champion for your calling or purpose *must* be you.

- Passionate commitment is necessary to signal your intent to the world so that the proper resources and people can participate in your cause.

Exercise for the Day

1. Make a list of the things (people, resources, experiences, etc.) that you need to remain focused and committed to your vision.
2. Prioritize the list so that the most important items are clear for the fulfillment of your vision and plan.
3. Tell your known supporters of your needs and desires – watch how things begin to happen to move you closer towards your hopes and dreams.
4. Recite the following prayer:

God I thank you for giving me a vision and a purpose in my life. I am committed to seeing _____ through. Surround me with the people, the resources and the desire to complete _____ . Please remove any negative thought, action or deed from my life so that my vision and purpose will be fulfilled according to Your purpose.

CHERISH YOURSELF AND THE EXPERIENCE

*"Nothing is predestined: The obstacles of your past can become
the gateways that lead to new beginnings."*
Ralph Blum

Focusing on past circumstances and experiences can often weigh us down so much that we are unable to enjoy the present and focus on the future possibilities. We stay on the "What if" street of life, constantly replaying a scene or situation to analyze what might have been. This keeps us stagnant and unable to move forward. Acknowledging the past, including the hurts and hardships, will allow us to move on to enjoy the present and be hopeful of the future. In the book <u>Do One Thing Different</u>, Bill O'Hanlon reminds us that, "The past certainly has an influence on us. But we don't have to let the past write the story of our future or have it make us act any certain way in the present."

O'Hanlon further suggests that regardless of a situation we always have the ability to shift the power to the person who can make the most difference – ourselves. By focusing on our inner power we would realize that we have the power to change any situation. It requires breaking out of what seems normal or traditional to us. We have to see things as we want them to be and not as they are. It requires us to stop hitting the rewind button as if it has the last say on who we are.

Additionally, if we truly want to gain the most from any negative experience we must practice forgiveness to others and to ourselves. When someone has wronged us or if we carry around our own guilt, we hinder our growth unnecessarily. The gift of forgiveness can be what liberates us. Ellis Cose, in his book Bone to Pick: Of Forgiveness, Reconciliation, Reparation and Revenge, suggests that the person wronged has the power to decide when and who to forgive. He states that, "forgiveness is a gift not only to the person forgiven but to those who grant the gift, those strong enough to forgive."

The strength inherent in forgiveness helps to free us forever from the past. It gives us power that enables us to cherish the experience and ourselves. It is a reminder that whatever happened to us is just one incident and it doesn't define us – unless we let it. Cose also suggests that holding on to the past and not practicing forgiveness bounds us to living in a cage. As such, he suggests one do "whatever it takes to remove one from that cage." This means we must forget the wrong or the need to be right and focus on moving forward. This elevates us from the cycle of pain we may be experiencing. At some point we must choose freedom or bondage. If freedom is our choice then forgiveness must be a part of that process.

This implies that we have a choice for what we want in our lives. Marianne Williamson in her book, The Gift of Change: Spiritual Guidance for a Radically New Life suggests that "We can have a grievance or we can have a miracle; we cannot have both." I suggest that we choose the miracle and recognize that everything we experience helps to shape us.

Be thankful for the experience. Cherish it and use it in the next chapter of your lives. The spirit of gratitude opens you up to feel more and receive more. Certainly, the experience, whether positive or negative, ensures that as Marianne Williamson suggests, we "… are further prepared for service to God."

"A Wonderful Change Has Come Over Me" – Pat's Story

The O'Jays had a popular song in the 70s called "Living for the Weekend." When I was growing up in rural North Carolina, the last thing I wanted at my house was the weekend. My father was an alcoholic and very abusive. Every weekend became a form of hell's pit. When he came home intoxicated, we never knew what to expect. He would throw food out of the house, fight my mother, beat my brothers or disturb the neighbors. By Sunday he would cool down in preparation for work.

My father was never affectionate and that was confusing to me. At the beginning of the week, he would be nice, but by weekend he would change and start acting like a monster. He seldom attended church but made my siblings and I attend Sunday school. Afterwards, he would treat us to a movie. My father was a hard worker and he taught my older brothers good work ethics, but chose not to adequately provide for his family. Instead he spent his money on beer and liquor.

This constant cycle of pain and confusion got the best of me and I began to develop a deep hate for him. I just couldn't understand how my mother could stay with a man who beat her repeatedly. He constantly blackened her eyes and busted her lips. He even broke her arm and cracked her skull, which required her to have surgery. Witnessing this caused my young heart of love to turn into a cold heart of stone.

When I was 14 or 15 my father was at work as a logger and a tree fell on him. My mother was told that he had a serious injury and may not survive. I hated my father so much; I prayed and asked God to "Let him die." In my "narrow" mind, I thought if he just died the abuse would stop and my family would benefit from his social security. Then my mother would be able to take care of the family.

My prayer was not answered; my father survived. Instead, God began to work on my attitude. The accident left my father paralyzed from the waist down and he was sent to a county-run nursing home. My brother and I went to visit him. The residents had a look of loneliness, hurt and neglect on their faces. I sensed it was a place that you sent people who were abandoned or not loved. As much as I hated him, I didn't want my father to remain there.

Without consulting my mother, my brother and I pushed my father in a wooden wheelchair over 2 miles on a dusty, dirt road to our house. When we arrived, I took the lead and walked in and asked my mother if my father could stay. I told her I would take care of him. I didn't know what to expect but I knew that my mother was a kind and compassionate person. To my surprise, she said yes and told us to put him in the front bedroom, which was the largest and best bedroom in the house.

My mother and I became the primary caregiver to a man that had never demonstrated any affection to any of us. My mother demonstrated love, kindness and prayer as a weapon against evil. I saw a change come over my father during this time. He humbled himself and was thankful for all that we were doing for him. Over the years my father had given each of us nicknames and for whatever reason he changed mine to "Good Girl." This unfortunate situation helped develop a bond between us. I never envisioned this since I had so much hatred towards him.

After I graduated from high school, I left home to attend business school in another state. It became difficult for my mother to maintain my father's care so she transferred him to a nursing home where he stayed until his death.

Even though I was married and living in a different state, I made frequent trips to check on his care, talked to him on the phone and sent him care packages. His physical health did not improve, but he began to do something I hadn't seen before. He responded to the church ministries that visited the nursing home.

During one of my visits he told me "Good Girl, I don't drink beer and liquor or smoke cigarettes anymore." On another visit he instructed me to go home and "Tell your mother and the others that I am sorry." I saw a man who had been meaner than anyone I had known ask for forgiveness. I forgave him and didn't realize then the effect it would have on me. Caring for him was the first step and forgiving him was the second. Once I accepted my father's apology and forgave him, God lightened my heart and renewed my spirit. To God I give the glory for the great things he has done in my life!

As I reflect on that time in my life I realize that hate is a slow death. It destroys you internally and can have lasting effects that can manifest itself in your outward appearance. Despite the turmoil my father wreaked on our household, I was able, with the help of the Lord, to move forward with my life. My mother amazed me too. With all the violence and beatings she endured, her love, strength and fortitude kept the family together. She never demonstrated any hate towards my father. I never heard her say degrading words against him and when he asked for forgiveness, she forgave him. I made the decision early in my adult life to cherish those experiences and make them a stepping-stone to a better life. I gave my heart and soul to God and my life has not been the same. Forgiveness changed me for the better.

"Nothing Will Keep Me From Living" – Dianne's Story

When I was 9 years old, my 16-year-old cousin locked me in his bedroom, blindfolded me and tied me to his bed. My brother came looking for me, but it was too late. The damage had already been done. My cousin raped me and offered me a measly 25 cents to keep quiet. This incident haunted me for the next 40 years.

My brother told my parents and my cousin was beaten very badly. After that no one spoke of it again except my cousin who asked for his quarter back the next day. From that day on, I no longer felt good enough or pretty enough. I felt ashamed that this happened to me. Nothing seemed to go right for me. I married at an early age to someone who was addicted to drugs and the marriage ended quickly in a divorce. Later, a man followed me home and raped me. I became pregnant as a result. More shame. How could this happen to me again?

After my son was born, I became very promiscuous and began a sexual affair with someone 10 years my junior. This too resulted in a pregnancy. The news of being pregnant again caused me to have a nervous breakdown. I was troubled on all fronts, but not ready to address the root of my pain. I committed myself to a mental hospital and slept with a Bible under my pillow. After one week, I was released from the hospital. I was very depressed but was encouraged by my minister's wife to have the child. She told me that having an abortion was not a choice, because I didn't know how the Lord might use the child. I decided to take her advice and became a single mother with two sons. I felt more shame. How could I now have two children and no husband?

I desperately felt I needed a husband and father for my sons and me. I married a man I thought would make a difference in our lives. After moving to another state, the marriage began to deteriorate. At the age of 39, I had a stroke and my husband told me "I was lucky because he was about to leave me." He stayed through the illness but he eventually left a few months later. After a few more reconciliations, he left for good. A couple of years later I saw him getting married on television to a much younger woman. Again, I asked myself – "Why Me?"

Prior to seeing him getting married, I had trouble letting go of the relationship. I kept thinking he would come back, be my husband and a father to our children. This didn't happen and the wedding became a turning point for me. I had to start taking responsibility for getting rid of my shame. I had to start liking and loving myself. I needed to give myself the worth that I deserved. I had to stop looking for validation in all the wrong places. I focused on going to school and became happy with me.

One of the hardest things I had to do was to forgive myself. I had been carrying around guilt and shame for far too long and those bags were getting heavy. The next thing I had to do was forgive my cousin. It was time for me to let go of everything. I called him and he told me he never forgot how he hurt me. He was constantly depressed and abusing alcohol. At the end of our call, he thanked me for setting him free.

Whenever I tell people what I have been through, they can't believe it. God has helped me through it all. Days have been dark, but God has worked on me. I'd been hurting internally for so long and couldn't see it. God has helped me face and appreciate what I have been through. I'm not sure why these things happened to me, but it doesn't define what I am working to become. Through it all, I can still smile and live in harmony.

"Committed to Me" – Kim's Story

My friends were getting married and told me I was being "too picky" with my men. They told me my standards were "too high." Society told me that I was getting older and needed to settle down. Instead of following my own instinct and the words of my mother – "true love doesn't hurt", "don't expect a man to make you happy, you can only make yourself happy," I married a man – the wrong man. I cried during the entire ceremony and it wasn't clear to me at the time if these were tears of joy. How did I marry the wrong man? How did I ignore all the signs?

While dating we had a lot of fun together – always going out of town alone –trips to the beach, crabbing, boat rides and more. He made me laugh, held doors open for me, prayed before eating and treated his mama well. I thought I had found the perfect man and I married him. We moved into our new home just four days later. I thanked God for blessing me with a new husband and a new home. By the fourth month of our marriage, certain behaviors and activities began to surface. I had completely missed things during our dating that would constantly remind me of the mistake I made.

We were newlyweds but never alone. He worked at night and I worked during the day. Every evening when I came home there would always be someone there with him talking and drinking. When I complained, he had his friends bring their wives to "occupy" me. I didn't notice the behavioral change so I wasn't suspicious. However it quickly became obvious that drugs and alcohol were a big part of his life. When I confronted him he would shell up and deny he had a problem. His response was "I only do it recreationally," "I'm not addicted to anything," or "I only do it when I feel like it." He would sleep on the couch in the basement to avoid any confrontations. He began to stay out all night, saying he was upset and needed to "clear his head."

Then his "baby mama drama" surfaced. His child's mother would stop by our house in the wee hours of the morning to collect daycare money, discuss their child or anything to annoy me. She disrespected me more than one time and my husband didn't seem to think there was a problem. This was more than I could take. After 8 months of marriage, I had enough. At this point, I was more concerned about me and my well being. My eyes were finally opened. Although I loved him and it was one of the hardest decisions I've ever made, I realized that he was not the man for me. He had revealed himself, finally removing his mask. I didn't care about the house, the idea of being married or what people would say. I had to focus on me.

I filed for divorce and began to commit some much needed time to me. For five years I didn't date anyone and it was the best thing I could have done. I really needed that time to regroup and reflect. I definitely recommend women taking time out for themselves, especially after experiencing a bad relationship. I learned a lot about myself — how strong I am and that I love myself enough not to let any man destroy my spirit. Although, this was the most disappointing situation I have ever experienced, I realized that I could forgive myself for the mistake I made and move on. I did and life is good!

"Not a Throwaway But a Precious Gift" – Crystal's Story

What can be said about a child born too early by man's standard? What can you say about a child who grew up surrounded by secrecy? What can you say about a child who didn't meet her birth mother until age 25 (and even then under a bit of deceit) or had never met her birth father? While man might look at the situation and call it one thing, God has always smiled on my life and called it something else – simply a gift.

I have always questioned my being, because my life has been based on lies, secrets and cover ups. Growing up and not knowing my birth father or mother had a tremendous effect on me. The only reason I met my birth mother was because my grandmother lied and told her I was in the hospital dying. I actually was there for corrective surgery. The incident left me wondering if she would have come under any other circumstance.

I have never met my birth father. People tell me that I get my musical talents and appearance from him. Yet, no one can tell me any other information about him. Where does he live? Is he dead or alive? What is his nationality? Does anyone have at least a picture of him? The only thing I know is that I have two siblings and that I am the oldest.

So many obstacles were placed in my path after my premature birth that I am certain that only God provided a means for me. As a child, I was slow in reading and math but excelled in other areas. Based on this, my family and high school counselor thought I should get a job instead of attend college. I have suffered abuse both as a child and as an adult and have felt like giving up. Others gave up on me, but God had a different plan for my life. When I couldn't keep myself, He stepped in and wrapped His arms around me.

I had dreams as a child that God would allow me to see come to fruition. I had to trust that despite my background, good things would happen for me. Eventually good things did happen for me. I was able to go to school and get a college degree. I have a loving and caring husband. I have stepsons and grandchildren. I have a great church home where a solid foundation has been instilled and most importantly, I have learned how to be patient.

God doesn't operate on my time but according to His will. Through faith, prayer, praise and worship, I have come to know that despite everything that has happened to me, I am stronger for it. God is my saving grace. He is the mother and father that I never had. I have learned to be thankful for my experiences. These experiences have shaped me into the person I am today. Where others may have viewed me as a throwaway, I now know my life is a gift to be used for His glory.

Lessons Learned

- The past does not influence our present or our future.

- Forgiveness is as much a gift to ourselves as it is to the person whom we forgive.

- A spirit of celebration and thanks regardless of the circumstances allows us to build on the experience.

Exercise for the Day

1. Write a letter of forgiveness to yourself or someone (Mailing it is not a requirement). Explain your hurt, offer forgiveness and then release it. Begin to experience the gift of forgiveness in your life.
2. Keep a journal and record all that you are thankful for – focus on what you have instead of what you don't have.
3. Recite the following prayer:

Lord, I thank you for this experience and where you have placed me in life. I count it not a mistake on your part. I choose a miracle in my life and God you are the architect of miracles. I ask that you allow me to experience Your greatness and use this experience to strengthen me for better service to You.

CONTINUE

"My barn having burned to the ground, I can see the moon."
Chinese proverb

Keep going. Don't quit. These are indeed simple concepts. However, in the midst of a difficult situation, we quickly forget what most of us have learned since childhood. Yet these are powerful, useful tools to navigate successfully through a trial. Bill O'Hanlon's book <u>Do One Thing Different</u>, recounts a tale of an ancient Buddhist principle. The story is of a traditional ceremony that exists every 100 years within the Buddhist religion. The ceremony involves students entering a room. The door through which they enter has no doorknob on the inside so they can't exit from it. Once inside the room students are forced to face their own demons and fears. If they chose to do this they could emerge from the room enlightened. The student and their course of action determine the timing and success of the enlightenment. Important advice from The Dalai Lama says, "Keep your feet moving. If you keep your feet moving, you will eventually get to the other side, find the door and come out."

That story succinctly summarizes the concept of "continue." We will face many obstacles in our lives – it's part of our own growth and development. We may or may not see the situation developing and at times, there isn't anything we can do to stop it from happening. And honestly, that's not what's relevant. It's not the test; it's our performance that counts. In the midst of a personal storm, the most important thing we can do is not to give in to negative messages or forces. Continuing is a prerequisite to clearing any circumstance successfully. There is absolutely no other option.

According to Marianne Williamson "...when the skies are darkest we get our best view of starlight." She further states, "All of us are passing from one state to another all the time and God sends guides and angels, inspirers and mentors, to light our way. He is always, always, preparing new life." This means that what we frequently view as death or an end may actually be absolutely necessary in order for God to prepare us for something new.

Therefore, there is no need to fight the situation or a potential change. It actually may be more detrimental to do so than to simply let things take their course. Remember the beautiful butterfly comes after an ugly existence as a caterpillar. And yet this change into a new, beautiful life doesn't occur immediately. What this means is that we too must resist the temptation to rush through an experience or change too quickly. There is a lesson we need, a message we must carry, a *"test"* developing for our testimony.

The possibilities of a new life should always be at the forefront of our thoughts as we encounter certain experiences. We should be anxious to see what's next. What does God want us to do now that we've had this experience? And in doing so, we continue with the hope and excitement of what the new day will bring.

"Only One Set of Footprints" – Linda's Story

In 1985, I was ill prepared for what I had to face. A collection of events, one after the other, seemed overbearing – divorce, injury, sickness, hospitalization, death and birth. I didn't know if I was equipped to handle them.

As the only girl in my family, I am frequently called upon to be a caregiver. Yet when I needed care myself, I had to stand tall and deal with all of these life-changing events within the family.

First, I had to deal with a nasty divorce. My husband left me for a woman 20 years his junior, which caused me to have to relocate back to my hometown for more affordable living. I was also out of work from a back injury. My only child was expecting my first grandchild. These incidents left me with a range of emotions– anxiety, joy, uncertainty, disappointment, and pain.

By October of that year, my grandchild was overdue and my father was entering the hospital for heart surgery. I tried hard to help my daughter "walk" the baby down but that old wife's tale didn't work and I had to leave her to be with my father. I asked my daughter not to have the baby until I could return, but she delivered the baby the same day of my father's surgery. Once I was sure my father was doing well, I headed back to Maryland to see my first grandchild.

As soon as I arrived, I received a call that my brother had been hospitalized. Momma called me from Daddy's hospital room and told me to get on a plane to Oklahoma because my brother needed a family member there to make decisions regarding his care – his situation was touch and go. I faced a tug of war– I was in Maryland with my grandbaby and daughter; Daddy was in NC recovering from surgery and Momma wasn't able to leave him. Since there wasn't another surrogate to go, I left Maryland for Oklahoma.

I stayed in Oklahoma until my brother moved from ICU to a regular room. My brother was dying and wanted to come home to North Carolina.

Before heading back to Maryland, I made arrangements for one of my other brothers to come to Oklahoma to pick him up. I was only there for two days when the call came that my brother had died. I headed back to NC to make funeral arrangements. During all of this, I wasn't taking good care of my own injury and making my doctor's appointments. My dress size went from a size 10 to a size 7 and I was frequently in pain. Any one of these situations is stressful enough but I was dealing with multiple life events all within a one-month period. My doctor commented that with me he wasn't sure if my glass was half full or half empty.

As I look back now, I know that despite all that was coming at me, I had no option but to continue. As the only girl of seven children I was used to being the "go to" person and duty called. Whether I felt equipped, prepared or not, life was happening all around me. Now this is where Philippians 4:13 "I can do everything through him who gives me strength" really comes through. Now that I am on the other side of that trial, I discovered what a strong person I really am. I realized that you can recover from any kind of setback. The secret is to put your faith and trust in God and let Him see you through.

October 1985 brought real meaning to the poem which references one set of footprints in the sand. God was carrying me through that point of my life. Now when trouble comes my way, I simply straighten my back, hand everything over to Him and continue. There is no choice except to ride out the storm because nothing lasts forever. The rain will come but after that - the rainbow appears.

"I'm Still Here" – Carol's Story

Sometimes you never know what to expect from life. We all plan things but sometimes there are detours and bumps in the road. I've learned from a major detour to appreciate all that life has to offer you. We all go through trials and tribulations, but some of these trials build character and give us strength and courage. In January 2004, I went for a routine mammogram and had to retake it twice. The radiologist came in and stated I needed a needle aspiration. A couple of days later, I received the results — irregular cells were found which required a tissue biopsy.

On January 31, 2004 (my 60th birthday), I was diagnosed with breast cancer. Well, "Happy Birthday to me". Breast cancer was a major ordeal for me. I went through six months of chemotherapy and nine weeks of radiation. Fortunately, I continued to work. I was not nauseous and only experienced minor discomfort. My family was very supportive. My husband took me to every chemo treatment and every radiation appointment (5 days a week for 9 weeks).

I retired in June 2005 after 33 years with the same company. I was now ready for the good life. My plans were to travel, read, shop, and participate with several interests groups (knitting and a travel group from church.) But my plan was not God's plan. I was still going to the oncologist every 3 months and by June 2006 my CA125 started to rise. After a MRI, CAT scan, etc., I was diagnosed with ovarian cancer. The ports were inserted under my breast and chest, which delivered the chemo directly to my abdomen. However, nothing about the treatment was easy this time. The drugs for ovarian cancer caused every bad side effect possible. With the support of my praying family and friends, I weathered another storm. I said my own prayers day and night and embraced each new day God provided me. I would awake and say, "It's a day the Lord has made, let me rejoice and be glad in it."

Despite, all that I have been through, the support of my family, friends and prayer have been my sustaining grace. God saw fit for me to come through this storm. I don't know the reason why He chose me for this path but I do know I'm a stronger woman for it. Who is wearing what or who said what is not important. What is important is to try to lead a good life, be kind to everyone, and try to help others. Each day there is a new opportunity to start again. So regardless of what I've endured, I'm still here.

"Is This the Ending or the Beginning?" — Harriett's Story

There's an old saying "What's done in the dark will come to light" and this was true in my relationship with my first husband. Twelve years after he had an affair that produced a child, I found out about it. This rocked my world and to me it was like it happened that day. I put my husband so high on a pedestal that I refused to believe that he was capable of committing adultery. All I could see in this man was that he was loving, caring and a great provider for my children.

I am strongly against adultery so when I found out about the affair, it really shook me up. Just the thought of him sharing what I thought was mine made me nauseous. I knew in my heart that this would tremendously affect my relationship with him. I told him that it would never be the same and that I wanted a divorce right then and there. However, I tried to hold onto my marriage for my children's sake but that didn't work. When we made love, all I could envision was my husband making love to his other woman and that made me feel violated.

While I was trying to hold things together, I was dealing with feelings of betrayal and hurt and I guess my husband was dealing with guilt. That started the mental and physical fighting. The fact that my eyes were opened now and I would no longer accept anything he said caused problems in the marriage. In the past I had relied on my husband for guidance because I loved and trusted him. However, his deceit caused my feelings of trust and admiration to erode. Without trust in a relationship, daily living can be a horrible experience. I felt "damned if I did and damned if I didn't". What were people saying? What would they think? Should I go or stay?

My situation was getting the best of me and I wasn't myself and started acting unlady like. I came from a good family and was not proud of the way I was acting. The way I responded to my husband's adultery was not only affecting me but my children. I felt as though I had started a journey with a roadmap but then was left standing in the middle of the road alone. I knew right then and there that I had to make some decisions on what to do with my unhappy life. I called on Jesus to help me sort everything out. To move forward, I needed strength and courage to face my situation and to move on. He answered my call.

I thought my life as I knew it was over, but I was wrong. The affair, the fights, the breakup and the pain were in fact an ending but also my beginning. I began to think and rely on myself to get through situations and found out that I am a survivor. With God's help, I was able to stand strong and do what I felt a woman must do – I took care of my children. God's grace and mercy saw me through a dark period in my life. I am much happier with myself and the choices I make. God continues to shower me with His goodness. For that I am humbly grateful. I have learned that what we think is an ending is just God's way of preparing us for something better. We have to accept it, trust God and continue. He has ordered the steps already anyway. We just need to be obedient and follow them.

"The Ultimate Test" – Gerri's Story

I've frequently questioned my purpose in life. The experiences I've had have been numerous – a few of them traumatic and yet I'm still here. I am a breast cancer survivor. I lost my mother to breast and lung cancer. I supported my sister in her fight with breast cancer and was there with my husband when he experienced his quadruple bypass surgery. My experiences have allowed me to "witness" to others facing a fight with cancer or a difficult life experience. They have also strengthened my relationship with God, so much that my brother teases me saying that I chase after Jesus Christ the way I used to chase after Marvin Gaye.

While I am thankful for the experiences and how they have shaped my life, nothing could have prepared me for the events of June 20, 2006. My daughter Monique was fatally wounded in a car accident on that day. Just two days before her death, her father and I met Monique, her husband Frank and their son Christian for Father's Day. The next day was Frank's birthday and they had gone out of town to celebrate. Monique was so happy about the wonderful time they had. I had no reason to believe that these would be her last days with us. She was only 40.

The day we lost Monique, my grandson called me on my cell phone while I was at a doctor's appointment. He said "Nana can you come to my house now?" Unfortunately, the patrolman was there and proceeded to tell me by phone (and in front of my 10-year old grandson) that my daughter had been killed in a car accident and he couldn't leave my grandson alone. A 2-ton dump truck struck Monique's SUV and sent it skidding into a swamp. She was killed instantly. I thank God that she did not suffer.

Monique was a unique and special person. She was active in her community. She was the vice president of the PTA and worked with the Parents Advisory Board. She was actively involved in her son's life and was always willing to provide information and opportunities to her employees at the bank she managed.

Oddly enough, just months before Monique's death, I had a strong urge to give her a 40th birthday party. I knew that wasn't her style and her husband and I worried about her response to such a big affair. We surprised her and fortunately she was a gracious hostess to friends and family - some of whom she hadn't seen in more than 20 years. She was extremely happy that night. As I reflect back, I couldn't understand why I was so adamant about giving her the party but I am happy she was able to get her "flowers" that day.

Some days I don't believe it is real. I keep thinking that it was just a horrible dream. I keep looking for her to come through the door. I have even questioned my own selfishness for not having more than one child. I wondered if it would hurt less if I had more children? There are people who say to me they know how I feel. I can only respond, "No you don't and I hope you never find out."

Despite my loss, I am thankful. I am thankful for the 40 years that Monique was a part of my life. I am thankful for the family that remains with me – a loving husband, my grandson who is the light of my life, a son-in-law who is like a son, a sister and two brothers and so many more family and extended family. God has smiled on me in a special way and my experiences only serve to allow me to be a witness to others who will travel a few of my paths. My purpose, therefore, is to help and encourage other people to get through similar, unfortunate situations. My ultimate test, the loss of my only child, solidifies more than ever God's existence in my life. I miss my daughter more than anyone will ever know but I remain comforted by one of her favorite quotes "If God takes you to it, He will bring you through it." Because He continues to walk with me daily, I continue.

Lessons Learned

- Death or "an end" doesn't always mean there's nothing more to expect. It could signal new life and experiences for us.

- God will always make provisions for new life. We should anxiously look forward to the next chapter of our lives.

Exercise for the Day

1. Reflect on the experiences you thought were the darkest. How did you make it? What worked best for you?
2. Add to your journal the strengths you gained as a result of that experience and the "newness" in your life that resulted from it.
3. Recite the following prayer:

   God I thank you for each and every experience in my life, the lessons You taught me and the strength I've gained. I thank You that in the midst of my endings, I see new beginnings. I thank You for bringing me to it and seeing me through it

EPILOGUE

The winds are blowing and your storm feels rough

Caught you off guard, wondering why life is so tough

Things seem great but can so quickly change

In the blink of an eye your life is rearranged

Everything that you know seems like a distant memory of the past

You're in a situation so deep you forgot not all things will last

But if freedom rarely comes to us free

Then we must face what we must and fight the need to flee

No need to fret – worrying into the midnight hour

Simply Choose2Change – You've got the power!

With God on your side there is no reason to fear

Just breathe deep, seek Him and then "C "your way clear

- Toya L. Evans (2007)

BIBLIOGRAPHY

Brinkman, Rick and Rick Kirschner.
Life by Design: Making Wise Choices in a Mixed-Up World. New York.
McGraw-Hill: 1999

Britten, Rhonda.
Fearless Living: Live Without Excuses and Love Without Regret. New
York, Penguin Group: 2001

Chodron, Pema.
When Things Fall Apart Heart Advice for Difficult Times. Boston,
Shambhala: 2003

Cose, Ellis.
Bone to Pick: Of Forgiveness, Reconciliation, Reparation and Revenge.
New York, Atria Books: 2004

Jones, Laurie Beth. Jesus CEO: Using Ancient Wisdom for Visionary
Leadership. New York, Hyperion: 1995

O'Hanlon, Bill. Do One Thing Different. New York, William Morrow
and Company Incorporated: 1999

Klauser, Henriette Anne, PhD.
Write It Down, Make It Happen: Knowing What You Want and Getting It.
New York, Scribner: 2000

Lucado, Max. Grace for the Moment: Inspirational Thoughts for Each Day
of the Year. Nashville, J. Countryman: 2000

Roulac, Ann Nichols. Power, Passion and Purpose: 7 Steps to Energizing
Your Life. Larkspur, California, Green Island Publishing: 2006.

Troccoli, Kathy. Live Like You Mean It: Seven Collaborations to
Rejuvenate Your Soul. Colorado Springs, Waterbrook Press: 2006

Willamson, Marianne.
The Gift of Change: Spiritual Guidance for a Radically New Life. San
Francisco, Harper: 2004

Vanzant, Ilanla.
Yesterday, I Cried. New York, Simon and Schuster: 1998

ABOUT THE AUTHOR

TOYA L. EVANS is an author, speaker and businesswoman with an MBA from Howard University and a BSBA from George Washington University. Her experience spans over twenty years in marketing and strategic consulting with large corporations such as General Electric, Microsoft and America Online. Additionally, Toya has spent considerable time operating her own small businesses as well as consulting with other small business enterprises. Her goal is to use her business and life experiences to *enlighten* and *inspire* people to take a different perspective on their lives – to try something different, and to move out of their comfort zone – *Choose2Change*.

Family, friends and community service are important to her. Toya is the mother of two daughters and resides in Northern Virginia. She is a member of Mount Pleasant Baptist Church in Herndon, VA and Delta Sigma Theta Sorority, Inc. For more information, or if you would like Toya to speak at your next corporate, association or public event, please visit www.changethings2day.com or email: toya@changethings2day.com

Share C'ing Your Way Clear: Every Woman's Guide to Handling Life's Storms with your friends and family.

Check your local bookstore, online bookstore, www.changethings2day.com, or Order Here

___ YES, I want _____ copies of C'ing Your Way Clear: Every Woman's Guide to Handling Life's Storms (ISBN: 9780979447501) for $10.95 each

Include $4.90 shipping and handling for one book and $1.95 for each additional book. Virginia residents must include applicable sales tax. Payment must accompany each order. Allow 3 weeks for delivery.

My check or money order in the amount of $_____ is enclosed.

Please charge my __ Visa ___ Mastercard ___ American Express

Name:_____

Address:_____

City/State/Zip: _____

Phone:_____Email:_____

Card#:_____

Exp. Date:_____ Security Code:_____

Signature:_____

Printed Name:_____

Mail to: Haci Publishing PO Box 2111 Ashburn, VA 20146
Checks payable to Toya L. Evans